French Bulldogs

French Bulldogs

Jane Eastoe

Illustrations by Meredith Jensen

BATSFORD

First published in the United Kingdom in 2023 by
B.T. Batsford Ltd
43 Great Ormond Street
London WC1N 3HZ

An imprint of B.T. Batsford Holdings Limited

ISBN: 9781849948418

A CIP catalogue record for this book
is available from the British Library.

10 9 8 7 6 5 4 3 2 1

Reproduction by Rival Colour Ltd, UK
Printed in China by Leo Paper Products

Contents

French Bulldogs

Introduction

Bonjour, bonjour, bonjour, je suis un Bouledogue Français, or French Bulldog if you prefer. I am the sweetest, most comical, most loving dog you could ever hope to meet. I am a companion dog par excellence and am such a favourite that the Frenchie now ranks as the most popular dog in the USA and the second most popular in the UK.

So what is the reason for my recent meteoric rise in the ratings? I am a very loving dog. You, my owner, are the source of my happiness and comfort, you are my security blanket. When I am with you all is right with the world! I am

happy for you to pet me, to coddle and cosset me. I like to be close to you at all times. In my eyes you can do no wrong.

I am not much of a barker, so am not likely to upset your neighbours. I don't need a huge house or garden. I am small and relatively portable, though perhaps a bit weighty to hold for more than a minute or two. I am generally friendly, tolerant of small children and easy-going with most dogs. I don't have much of a prey drive, though I might make a fruitless attempt to catch a squirrel, and I live harmoniously with other pets.

I am not very demanding in terms of exercise and don't need you to tramp across the moor with me for hours, day in and day out. Two short walks a day are quite enough for me. My reputation as a couch potato is somewhat undeserved for I adore going out on my little walks. I love playing with other dogs and doing zoomies, but I can't keep going for long; after a short burst of activity I like to take a little rest and recover my breath.

I am quite clean and abhor getting muddy or wet. I will be perfectly happy to stay at home on the sofa when it is raining. My soft, velvety coat is short and easy to look after, but I do shed, and I need help in keeping the folds of my skin clean. A quick wipe over here and there just two to three times a week is sufficient, it keeps me smelling fresh and helps ensure I don't develop skin conditions. On the downside I can drool a bit and I slosh an awful lot of water around when I take a drink!

I am great fun to live with and my expressive face makes me a natural comedian. I have a broad grin but can also adopt a look of great tragedy. I love entertaining you and making you laugh. If you leave me alone I will shower you with gifts on your return – admittedly it's just my chewed up toys that I deposit so tenderly at your feet, but it's my way of demonstrating how important you are to me.

Mealtimes are one of the high points of my day, I may nag you to feed me as dinnertime draws close. I can emit a startling whining yodel designed to tug at your heartstrings and I can get quite sulky if you ignore my vocal demands. It's tempting to give in to me but stand firm, the more you indulge me the more demanding I will become.

On the subject of food, I may as well be upfront about its side-effects. My gaseous emissions are frequent and pungent. I fart, and I fart a lot! Proper, big, loud farts. Sometimes so loud they even startle me! I also snore a bit, but if you say my name, I may well shift position in my sleep to stop myself snoring. That's the clue as to where I like to sleep – with you, as close to you as you will let me get, and I am quite a weight on the bedclothes!

Like all other dogs you can train me to sleep on my own, but I've yet to meet a Frenchie owner who doesn't admit that slowly but surely their dogs have graduated to sharing their bedroom. If night after night you find us with our nose pressed against the bottom of your bedroom door, it's hard to resist inviting us in.

I love you so much that I struggle being parted from you. No dogs should be left for more than five hours at a stretch in the daytime, but that really is a bit too long for me. Fearing your desertion above all else I have a tendency to develop separation anxiety. If left alone as a pup I might display this anxiety in a spree of wanton destructive behaviour. I may also urinate or defecate in panic. If you can't give me a lot of your time I will need to spend time with other people so I can't fret.

My breed has British roots, was popularized and developed in France, before being tweaked, polished and defined in the USA. I am a descendant of the English Bulldog (itself a descendant of the Mastiff), bred for the blood sport of bull-baiting which was finally banned in Britain in the Cruelty to Animals Act of 1835. No longer serving a purpose, bulldogs were then crossed with other dog breeds to produce the smaller and friendlier toy or miniature bulldog.

The Toy Bulldog was introduced to France between 1815 and 1870, when thousands of artisan English lacemakers emigrated to Northern France where their work was in great demand and unaffected by the industrialization of their home market. These English lacemakers took with them their beloved Toy Bulldogs. The reasons for their particular fondness for this breed are unknown, possibly companionship or perhaps because they served as a welcome hot water bottle, being content to curl up on their owners' laps for hour after hour.

Either way, the French, and notably the Parisians, took these sturdy and affectionate little dogs to their hearts and demand for them rocketed. Café owners, butchers, bakers and street walkers were all seduced by the charms of this easy-going breed. French breeders developed a dog that was more uniform in look and it became known as the French Bulldog. The only issue of contention in the breed was whether the ears should stand up like a bat, or flop over in a rose shape.

Wealthy Americans on the Grand Tour were enamoured of these little French Bulldogs and exported them back to the USA. They became so popular that the French Bull Dog Club of America was founded in 1897. It published the very first breed standard for French Bulldogs and controversially defined the desired ear shape as bat. This caused something of a furore with French and English breeders, who preferred the rose ears, but the Americans won out and those distinctive bat ears became the only acceptable ear shape for us Frenchies.

The American Kennel Club gave official recognition to the breed in 1898, with The Kennel Club in Britain following suit in 1906. The breed's popularity began to decline after the First World War, but started climbing again in the 1980s, slowly rising to its current heights.

Our immense popularity is understandable; we are incredibly loyal and form a deep attachment to our owners and their wider family.

We don't need much space or much exercise and we're adaptable and easy-going. Give us a bed and we will curl up, preferably in the same room as you and sigh in contentment that we get to share our lives with the most wonderful people in the whole wide world, not that we are biased!

What must be acknowledged by anyone wanting to bring a French Bulldog into their life is that the development of our breed has led to a number of associated health problems, not least respiratory difficulties which can cause a range of complex issues. Please, only purchase Frenchies from reputable breeders so that these physical abnormalities can be minimized over time. This wonderful, loving dog deserves to be given the best future.

Bruce

Owned by Shannon and Adam | Lives in Squamish, British Columbia
@brucethefrenchbully

A larger-than-life personality.

Puppies

I don't like to brag, but when it comes to puppies there really is nothing more adorable than a French Bulldog puppy! Our fur is soft and our skin too big for our small bodies so we have wrinkles and folds everywhere. Our eyes are huge and our bat ears comical and expressive. Perhaps our most seductive feature is that we not only love you, but worship you. You are EVERYTHING to us, we want to be with you the whole time and the fact that your mere presence makes us so ecstatically happy is a boost to your ego – who doesn't appreciate being hero-worshipped?

However, sometimes we are too adorable for our own good. Our owners can be inclined to baby us, but we are not babies! We are dogs and we need to be treated as dogs. We should not be indulged and spoilt because we can be incredibly stubborn over some things such as the time we are fed. We push to get our own way, we talk back big time! I understand all too well that I am hard to resist, but it is essential that you kindly and gently teach me how to behave right from the start. If you indulge us too much you are simply making a rod for your own back.

When we are small we are easy to pick up and carry, but be warned, our centre of balance is heavily weighted to our front end, so we are easy to accidentally drop. Please don't allow children to pick us up for this very reason. Encourage children to sit on the floor and then we can climb on to their laps. This way we both enjoy the cuddle.

We are a brachycephalic, or flat-muzzled breed and our cute looks come at a physical cost: we are predisposed to some anatomical defects, which can affect our health and welfare, not least breathing difficulties and problems with heat regulation (Health and First Aid). Only buy a French Bulldog puppy from a reputable breeder who is using DNA tests and screening schemes to help reduce the impact of a range of physical disorders from their litters. Reputable breeders will be registered with the Kennel Club of that country and with connections to the breed club.

When you come to meet us for the first time you will be questioned carefully by our breeder as to what you want from us. Do you want a show dog or a pet? What kind of a pet do you want, loving or lively? According to your answers you may only be shown a couple of puppies to choose from that best suit your requirements.

You should meet my mother and quite possibly some of my other relatives too. My father might not be around to see as he may live some distance away, but you should see a picture of him at the least.

A litter of French Bulldog puppies is adorable but let me give you some words of wisdom: even if you plan to have two dogs eventually, don't get them from the same litter at the same time, no matter how great the temptation. Frenchie puppies are a handful; we are playful, clumsy, strong, boisterous, we chew anything and everything and need masses of attention. If you take me and one of my siblings, we will become very reliant on each other and pay you little heed. What's more, as we mature, we may fight to determine which is the dominant Frenchie in the pack. A pair of male French Bulldogs are very likely to get territorial, which can cause no end of problems. If you want two Frenchies start first with one and only get a second when the first is well trained. The first dog will lead the way with all the basic training techniques.

We French Bulldogs can get a tad possessive of our owner and jealous of attention given to any other dogs in our home environment, even if we are fabulously sociable outside the home. So, while a second dog may seem like a good idea, if your Frenchie is jealous, possessive and insecure you might do better to stick with just the one to maintain a happy home environment.

Home preparation

Once a sale has been agreed you should make a few preparations.

Arrange to take a good chunk of time off work to help your puppy settle in. The more secure I feel from the start the better your chance of curtailing my tendency to separation anxiety. If you can't take much time off work, you will need to arrange for someone else to be with me. It is not fair to leave any puppies alone for long when small, but Frenchies really can't cope with being left alone for more than a few hours at a

time throughout their life. If you are out at work all day you will need to arrange for me to go to doggy day-care with someone, a friend popping in to let me relieve myself in the day is not sufficient.

However, it is important you still leave me for short spaces of time once I have got used to my new environment.

I will need a lovely soft bed, but you'll probably find that a big adult one may overwhelm me. Initially it is good to have something with nice soft sides so that I am protected from draughts. Soft cloth doughnut beds with tall sides – so I can rest my back against it as I did with my siblings – will suit me very well and help to keep me calm.

You might want to get me a crate to give me a nice safe bolthole. I will appreciate it if you cover this over with a blanket to stop draughts, put my bed in it and a heated pad to simulate the warmth of my siblings. If you put paper, or a puppy pad on the floor of the crate I can relieve myself in the night. I will not usually ever soil my bed, but accidents happen and when very small I will need to pee during the night. Please check my bedding in the morning to make sure it is dry – we like to have clean bedding, so wash it if it is wet.

You can shut the door of the crate at night, after I have been out for a pee. Then you can sleep easy in the sure knowledge that I can't run around in the night. In the daytime, it should not be used as a cage, although you can shut me in for short periods if you are going out.

Buy two bowls, one for food and one for water, which you leave down for me the whole time. Stainless steel is durable and easy to keep clean. Although Frenchies have short legs, we still benefit from our food bowls being on a low stand so that we are not bending down too much to get at our food and water. We are greedy and inclined to gobble, so a slow feeder bowl that makes us work to get at our food, is a sensible purchase.

You should also purchase a supply of poo bags so you can scoop my poop; compostable bags are available.

Please buy me some toys. I LOVE my toys. I will want to chew, and I am very playful. If I start to nibble or nip your fingers, you can give me a toy to chew on instead – my teeth are like needles! I will get the message that one is acceptable, and the other is not (see the chapter on training for more detailed advice). Soft toys are particular favourites – and I can be quite gentle with them. Harder toys are helpful for teething.

You may also want to get me a lightweight puppy harness and a lead, even though you won't actually be able to take me out for a walk for a few weeks. Until my vaccinations kick in, it is simply not safe for me to mix with other dogs, or to be anywhere that other dogs have been. However, please take me out and about with you in a carrier. You will be mobbed like a film star because I am just so cute; this is important socialization for me, but bear in mind that all this attention can be overwhelming.

Once I am old enough to go for walks, always make sure that you can slip two fingers underneath the harness and remember to check it regularly, I will grow quickly and tight harnesses are uncomfortable. If you put a harness on me early, and put me on the lead to play, I will get used to it before you take me out on my first walk.

House rules

It is a good idea to agree house rules in advance of my arrival. Am I going to have the run of the house, be limited to the downstairs, or only allowed in certain rooms under supervision? Am I going to be allowed on the sofa or the beds? As a dog with an oral fixation and a genetic tendency to obesity, a good rule would be to never give me treats from the table (please no!). I need consistency and clarity and will constantly challenge boundaries.

Please scour the house in advance for things that I might chew or eat that could be harmful. I am like a toddler and cannot be trusted to be sensible, quite possibly for the next two to three years!

The journey home

We Frenchie puppies usually leave our families at 12 weeks old. The extra weeks of interaction with our siblings help our socialization and confidence and for a breed that can fall prey to

Things to hide out of sight:

- Your shoes
- Your socks
- Electric wires, plugs and cables, your mobile phone, TV remote controls
- Children's toys
- Medicine or chocolate in your handbag or briefcase, or lying around
- Slug pellets, mouse traps and garden chemicals
- Painkillers
- Cleaning products – plastic bottles are very tempting to chew
- Your underwear – high embarrassment quotient when I appear with a pair of your pants in my mouth, plus I may eat them

anxiety it is worth the wait to make your puppy more secure. By this time I will be weaned, but be prepared, I may

come with a list of dietary requirements for the first few months and my breeder should give you some of the kibble I have been eating to help me settle in with you. This should help avoid tummy upsets. Please follow the breeder's guidance, Frenchies can have delicate tummies and suffer from allergies more than some other breeds, and you want your pup to have a smooth start with you. Vomiting or diarrhoea can dehydrate a puppy very quickly.

I will also have been microchipped, wormed and may have had my first inoculation. My breeder will give you my Kennel Club documents which have full details of my lineage.

The journey to my new home may be trying. Remember, I probably won't ever have been in a car, and I may cry for my siblings. I may be car sick, I might pee, or even poo. On the other hand, I might just fall asleep on your lap and stay that way for the whole journey. It is a good idea to have some old towels and some kitchen roll to hand so you can easily deal with all eventualities. You might even want to pack a change of clothes – don't wear anything precious!

If I am car sick, I will grow out of it. Long term, we Frenchies tend to be good travellers. If I am car sick as a puppy don't let me develop a phobia about the car. Keep putting me in it for a few minutes. Stay with me, give me treats. We don't need to go anywhere. Then take me round the block a few times on a short journey so I learn that being in the car is not a scary experience.

When we arrive home for the first time put me down in the garden to give me a chance to relieve pent up tensions! Stay with me!

Welcome

When you bring me into the house put me down and let me sniff around for a little while. Please don't overwhelm me with attention, especially if there are children in the house. Let me go to them and sniff them, let me take things at my own pace. This will be a scary experience for me. Show me my bed and some toys. Show me where my water bowl can be found. When I have had a little time give me something to eat, then take me outside straight away and give me the chance to do my business.

First night (start as you mean to go on)

Given the choice I will sleep with you, in your bed. I will be sad and lonely without my siblings and without you. I will cry, I may wail, and I even emit a noise like a curious yodel. If you can't cope with this, keep me close for a few nights until I have settled in. Some people tuck the puppy bed beside theirs for a few days, so that they can reach down and stroke us for reassurance. I will get used to sleeping by myself in time. Don't be surprised if I snore.

Most Frenchies I know wind up sleeping in their owners' bedrooms, even if they start off by sleeping elsewhere; over a period of time the owners get worn down and submit to their pooch's overwhelming longing to be close by at all times. We are 'companion' dogs after all!

Training basics

Training starts from day one, but before you leap to that chapter, make sure that everyone in your household grasps the basic principles. Agree as a household what specific training words you will use in advance; I will grasp clear, one-word instructions much faster. Use sit – not sit down; if you want me to lie down on the floor say down – not lie down; wait if you want me to stay in one place until summoned; stay – if you want me to remain still until you return to me; and leave if you want me to let go of something. I will also need a trigger word for going to the toilet, see below.

House training

Please familiarize yourself with the principles of house training a Frenchie in advance. Start collecting newspapers or buy puppy pads in preparation. It is much harder to house train any dog when the weather is cold, than when it is warm and doors can be left open all the time. Frenchies don't like the rain, so a Frenchie puppy may be quite resistant to staying outside when it is wet.

Don't leave me in the garden alone. I like to be with you so will only worry about where you've gone and not focus on peeing or pooing. Please stay out with me, that way you can praise me effusively when I do the deed.

While I am a puppy, I will probably want to pee every time I wake up from a sleep and also to pee and/or poo straight after every meal, so take me outside as much as you can. Every time I use the outdoor facilities I am making scents that will trigger a similar response next time. As a general rule I need to be taken outside every two hours as a minimum, hourly is even better. Try to stay outside with me for a bit after I have done my business, play and let us both have some fun – you are rewarding me for being good.

Agree on a key word you will use for toilet training – make this a word you don't use frequently in general conversation – my owner uses 'bumbles'! Use the agreed word when I am peeing or pooing, say it over and over again quietly and gently. Don't tell me that I am a 'good girl' or a 'good boy' as this may become my trigger phrase to urinate.

I will learn in time that when you use this trigger word you want me to pee or poo – such as last thing at night or before you leave me in the house when you are going out. If everyone in the household does this, I will learn what you want me to do much faster. Make a HUGE fuss of me every time I pee or poo out of doors, I need to understand that you are happy when I do this!

Make a mental note of where I like to pee outside and take me to that area when you want me to use the facilities. Some dogs like a dry surface such as gravel, stone or concrete, some will only pee on short grass, we all have our preferences.

At night I can last for about four to five hours without peeing. Some owners set an alarm to take their puppy out. Others keep one ear open and whisk us outside if they hear us wriggling. It all depends on where I am sleeping.

If I do have an accident don't shout at me. Say 'NO' loudly if you catch me in the act and carry me into the garden, then praise me effusively when I pee. Frenchies are sensitive to their owner's moods and hate to upset them; shouting will only frighten me and make me nervous. It might also make me hide away when I need to pee which will just compound the problem as you might not notice.

Gentle handling is required and lots of praise and rewards when I get things right. Frenchies are smart, I will catch on eventually. Clean up the accident area with an enzymatic cleaning material; biological washing powder mixed with warm water in a 1:9 ratio will remove all hint of a smell. If you don't do this I will always be tempted to return to the same spot. Household disinfectants should be avoided as they contain ammonia and the smell of this may encourage me to soil the same area again.

I'll be straight with you, even when we are fully house trained, we Frenchies can piddle with anxiety when left alone for a period of time - we just hate being separated from you. This can be an ongoing issue, so if you don't like coming home to a puddle, the simplest thing to do is to take me with you as much as possible or leave me with someone so at least I'll have some company.

Healthy eating

After the first night with me, it will be time to tackle my dietary requirements. My breeder should give you a sample menu and some of the packet food I have been eating to avoid any tummy upsets, from dietary changes. Don't change things around until I am settled. If you do change the make of food please do so gradually.

Frenchies are naturally greedy dogs, so I will usually gobble up every last morsel. If I don't eat, keep an eye on me, I may be unwell. Lift my food bowl up after ten minutes and don't offer me food until my next mealtime. If I am still not eating after 24 hours, you may need to get me checked out by the vet.

As a small puppy, I will need four meals a day, nicely spaced out please. By 12 weeks I can drop to three meals a day, and at six months I will be ready for just two meals a day. I will be fully grown from around 9-12 months, then I can go on to adult food as I will not require the same nutrients I did when I was actively growing.

Recall

Start working on this as soon as you have settled on my name. Have treats to hand. Call my name in a slightly higher pitched voice than usual and sound excited. When I come to you reward me with a treat and make a HUGE fuss of me. Let me go, then repeat. Stick to my name only - no other words, not here, not come, just my name.

Treats

Keep treats strictly for training purposes, don't give me anything off your plate, as much as I gaze at you with big round eyes. This will be hard because as I grow, I will become an expert in emotional blackmail. Try to remain resolute.

The vet

Most vets like you to register with them as soon as you get a puppy. They will give me a once over to check I am doing OK, weigh me, test my microchip, get my vaccination schedules in place and discuss flea and tick treatments. They will also make a fuss of me so that my first visit to the vet is a positive experience. Vets will probably know about puppy socialization classes in the area and usually have lists of useful

contacts for the future such as kennels and dog sitters.

The vaccination schedule varies slightly from country to country so be guided by your vet. Some diseases

The following vaccinations are required in most countries:

- Parvovirus
- Canine distemper
- Hepatitis
- Leptospirosis

require me to have an annual booster to ensure continued protection. The vet will advise you and will normally send out a reminder. All these diseases are extremely unpleasant and are easily passed on. Please make sure I am vaccinated as a puppy and that you maintain my annual booster jab schedule to keep me safe.

Keep your vaccinations certificates safe. The vet can update them as required and you will have to show

Rocco

Owned by Emilie | Lives in Leeds | @rocco_thebluemerle

Rocco is an adorable Frenchie with distinctive
Merle ears. He always puts a smile on people's
faces and loves to model as a dog influencer.

them if you need to put me into kennels. No reputable kennels can take an unvaccinated dog.

A rabies vaccination will be required if you intend to travel internationally with me. This is not a quick process; rabies vaccinations need time to become effective and I require blood tests to ensure I have sufficient immunity. Allow a minimum of six to eight months for this process. You will also need to ensure that I have annual rabies boosters.

Frenchie Fact

- **Famous Frenchie owners** include: Leonardo DiCaprio, Dwayne Johnson, Madonna, David and Victoria Beckham, Snoop Dog, Cesar Millan, Hugh Jackman, Reese Witherspoon, Eva Longoria, Martha Stewart, Tom Hardy and Marcus Rashford to name but a few.

Harness and lead

While I am in quarantine and have to be carried about in the big wide world, take the opportunity to get me used to both my harness and a lead. Be forewarned, I will not enjoy this experience. Start with the harness; put it on for a few minutes, give me treats, then take it off. Once I have had a few days to get used to the harness, try me with the lead. A few minutes at a time for both. Lots of treats please. While

I can wear a collar to carry an ID disk, never, ever, attach my lead to a collar. If I pull this will affect my airway and can compromise my ability to breathe.

Walking

I love to race around the garden and the house. Let me do this as much as I like because I have the choice to stop and rest whenever it suits me. However, please don't take me out on long route marches or expect me to accompany you on a jog. As a general rule, start with five minutes exercise a day, building up to a maximum of 60 minutes over the course of the day – two 30-minute walks daily is ideal. Overheating is a major issue for me, so please don't exercise me at the hottest time of day.

Puppies under three months don't need walks; their vaccinations haven't usually taken effect until this time anyway so it shouldn't be an issue, but please bear in mind that I am heavy and you don't want to stress my developing joints and bones. Increase the amount of exercise I get a day slowly so that you build my muscles and increase my stamina gradually. When I get to be a senior dog and start slowing down, you may have to shorten my walks.

Social niceties

All dogs benefit from puppy socialization as soon as their vaccination schedule permits and Frenchies especially so. We tend to be incredibly friendly but can suffer from anxiety so we need socialization classes even more. Be gentle with us; you might just need to sit and watch the class with us until we look sufficiently interested in the proceedings. Submissive peeing is quite common when we are little – it's just our way of showing that we know our place – so outside socializing might be a good idea.

When puppies mingle expect a lot of butt sniffing. For some reason you humans seem to find this ritual impolite, but it is simply our way of saying hello, so try not to mind. Please don't tell us off for doing what comes naturally. It also teaches us to recognize the signals that another dog might not be so friendly – if a strange dog stands with a stiff body and tail, with its hackles rising and ears back, I have to learn to back off.

Puppy socialization classes usually include some element of group training and teach me to focus on you even when there are lots of distractions around. The instructors will also teach you dog training techniques. Let's be frank about this, these classes are as much for you as they are for me. You have to learn how to handle me

effectively so I will behave beautifully for you. You might think I'll never learn how to do anything, but the dog trainer will show you, with terrifying ease, how easy it is to get me to do what you want.

Don't blame me if I behave badly; basically it's all down to you. Keep on with my training every day and just wait to see how smart I am. Remember, there are no bad dogs, just bad owners.

Remember to take poo bags with you and those high-status treats – lots of them – it will help to keep me focused on you and what you want me to do.

Nervous puppies

Most Frenchie puppies are quite bold and bumptious, but others suffer from anxiety.

It is very important that you take me around a range of situations: busy roads, stations, cafés and parks so that I can meet different men, women, children, dogs and get used to the strange noises around me. I need to see bicycles and wheelchairs, people in hats or carrying walking sticks, every experience will help me adjust to the wider world. Carry me if my vaccinations have not yet kicked in, don't wait to take me out with you.

If I am nervous of other dogs when I am old enough to go out and about, don't scoop me up out of harm's way. This will only reinforce the idea that I am in grave danger. Talk to other dog owners and ask if it is OK to stroke their pets and talk to them, but don't push me forward. Let me see you being open and friendly and let me build my confidence at my own pace.

Separation anxiety

All dogs are pack animals and are happiest when they have you, the pack leader, in their sights. We Frenchies are incredibly attached to our family and hate being left behind, so we can suffer from separation anxiety.

Try not to reinforce nervous behaviour from the start. If your puppy hates being away from you, encourage it to play, then leave the room for a moment, keep playing and popping back so they get more confident that you will return.

The same applies to teaching me to get used to being home alone. Only

leave me alone for a few minutes initially so I don't get the chance to panic. Tire me out before you leave so that hopefully I'll just fall asleep. Build up the time you leave me little by little, starting with just five minutes.

Give me a fantastic toy to play with, such as one filled with treats, so that I am kept busy and occupied and am not stressed because you aren't in sight. A Kong is very useful, you can fill the inside with meat and freeze it so that I have to work to release the lovely, tasty filling.

Many people allocate their Frenchie puppy a particular space in the house

Frenchie Fact
- **A French Bulldog named** Gamin de Pycombe went down with the *Titanic* in 1912. Her owner, a banker named Robert Williams Daniel, insured his beloved pooch for £150 (around £20,000 in today's money). The owner survived the sinking, but sadly his beloved Frenchie did not.

when they go out, stair gates will help to confine me and stop me wreaking havoc throughout the house. I also feel safe in small, confined spaces, having the run of the whole house can make me nervous when I am alone.

Dog charities recommend that no breeds are left alone for more than four to five hours at a stretch, French Bulldogs are even less tolerant, three hours may be as much as they can cope with. After all, we are a 'companion' breed and want to be with you. If you can't cope with that then a Frenchie simply isn't the right breed for you.

Frenchie Fact

- **Artist Toulouse Lautrec** highlighted the popularity of the Bouledogue Français when he drew and painted the characterful Frenchie Bouboule belonging to café owner Madame Palmyre.

Travelling companions

If you take your Frenchie puppy on public transport when I am small I may be fearful at first, but I will get used to it and behave calmly. Car travel, although you might not think it, has more restrictions.

In the UK, the Highway Code states that dogs and other animals must be suitably restrained. The interpretation of this is quite loose, however for your sake and mine, please ensure that proper restraints are in place. Quite apart from the fact that you adore me and don't want any harm to come to me if we have an accident, please remember that if I come hurtling through the car at speed I can kill you in precisely the same way another human can if they are unrestrained in the rear of the car.

The most effective way to keep me safe is to have a crate in the rear of your car to minimize the distance I can be flung in a crash. If you accustom me to the crate at home, I will be perfectly content to travel in this. Dog harnesses that clip on to seat belts can be utilized if a crate is not an option. These should not be used in the front seat because if an airbag goes off in an accident it could seriously harm your dog.

Hormones and bitches

As I move towards my first birthday and the end of puppyhood the hormones will already have kicked in; in developmental terms a one-year-old Frenchie is the equivalent of a 15-year-old human. Most female Frenchies will have their first season (proestrus) between the ages of six to nine months, but some can go into heat a little later than this.

Frenchie bitches tend to come into heat every six to eight months, however, the frequency of seasons can vary depending on when her first season begins. Please do not consider breeding a litter of puppies, this breed does not reproduce easily, and it requires the specialist expertise of a breeder to bring a litter of healthy French Bulldog puppies safely into the world.

Your bitch will be on heat for around 21–28 days. She may well become cranky and for good reason: her vulva will swell, her nipples may swell, she will bleed and she will also need to urinate more frequently. She will drop spots of blood and it will be hard for her to keep herself clean.

In this modern world you can now purchase pants for bitches on heat. She can wear these in the house, but she may take great exception to this addition to her wardrobe. You can cover her bedding and the sofa with towels and wash them regularly, and you can cover carpeted areas of the floor with towels or newspaper. You can clean spots as they appear and then have your carpet professionally cleaned when she has finished her season. Try not to let any irritation show, she will pick up on this.

Keep her in close contact when she is on heat; male dogs will find her irresistible and they can pick up her pheromone-filled scent from a long way away. Only let her off the lead when you can do so safely or choose to walk her at times of the day when there will be fewer dogs around to bother her.

If you also have a complete male dog in the house, your life is about to get very difficult. One option is to persuade a friend to look after your male dog until your bitch has finished her season, or alternatively keep your dogs apart. The use of stair gates or crates can allow the two dogs to still see each other, but not interact.

Some bitches can get very uncomfortable when they are on heat and a trip to the vet may be required. The vulva can become painfully swollen and she may be producing milk and will require medication to halt this.

Neutering your Frenchie bitch once she has had her first season will give her protection against some forms of cancer and infection of the uterus (pyometra). Speak to your vet about the best time to have her spayed. French Bulldogs are sensitive to anaesthesia and your vet will need to be alert to this problem. Your Frenchie bitch does not need a litter of puppies to be happy, indeed it is dangerous. Bulldogs have a narrow pelvis and the puppies' heads are large. Most Frenchie pups can only be born by caesarean section.

Hormones and male dogs

Most male Frenchies are fertile before they are fully grown, somewhere between eight and 12 months. The usual time to have your dog neutered is around six to eight months as the dog is entering puberty. The breeding of French Bulldogs should be left to specialist breeders, the responsible owner will have their dog neutered.

Just like teenage boys, male Frenchies sometimes act before they think, the testosterone is surging! In fact, for a short while, young male dogs have more testosterone than adult dogs and this can lead to a sudden outbreak of territorial behaviour. Scent marking territory is an early indication of sexual maturity: if your male Frenchie continually stops for short pees to signal where he has been, this is scent marking. You may also find to your horror that a perfectly house-trained Frenchie suddenly lets you down by peeing inside a friend's house, or in a shop, or a pub. This can happen with all breeds, not just Frenchies. Please always own up to my offence and offer to clean up my puddle.

Perfectly amiable Frenchies can suddenly start having stand-offs with other dogs. Don't panic, this doesn't necessarily mean your sweet boy is going to become an aggressive monster. Male dogs have to deal with a whole new set of signals from other males, who may suddenly be aggressive with them. Your puppy needs to learn to revaluate the social signals he is getting. He will learn.

If you are having to deal with some aggression for the first time, try not to panic. Reinforcing good behaviour will help. If you are struggling, seek help from a professional dog trainer.

Training

If you watch French Bulldogs out and about it is easy to get the impression that they are the best behaved dogs in the world. They trot happily along beside their owners, don't run away from them, don't lunge and bark at every dog they pass, don't chase sheep, rabbits or deer, and sit quietly in cafés like regular patrons. However, you should be aware in advance that you may have some training issues with us, not least because we can be pig-headed. If we don't want to do something we REALLY will try our level best not to do it. For this reason you need to be on top of training from the word go.

I tell you this because I want you to understand that Frenchies are not all well-behaved by nature; hard work on your part, and my character will influence my progress. However, the more you train me and keep me exercised and mentally stimulated, the happier I will be.

The fact that I am food-motivated is a plus. I don't have a long attention span so keep training sessions short and give me loads of fuss. Consistency and kindness in training right from the start will enable you to overcome any issues in time.

The basic rules
of dog training

- It is your job to keep me under effective control. You must have a lead with you every time we go out and use it when necessary to keep me safe on the roads, when signage requests it – often when nesting birds are in the vicinity – or around livestock. Never let me roam unsupervised.

- Don't let me approach cyclists, runners or other dog owners unless invited.

- Don't let me race off the lead across private land or through crops – this isn't usually a problem with French Bulldogs as we like to stay close to you, but nevertheless be aware.

- Never let me worry or chase livestock.

- Be safe around livestock. Check fields before entering so you are not caught unawares. Keep a good distance from livestock and give them plenty of space.

Cattle and horses can be quite curious of dogs and very protective if they have calves or foals. If livestock comes worryingly close release me so that I can get away and you can too.

- Always bag up my dog poo and take it with you; this can be disposed of in special dog poo bins or if none are around, any public litter bin.

- Don't leave bags of poo on the path to pick up later or hang them from branches of trees. It is too easy to forget them or lose them. Pick up as you go.

- Put an identification tag on my collar with your contact details on it. Put your name on it (not my name) and a phone number. Remember to update this and my microchip details if we move home.

- Keep my vaccination and worming treatments up to date.

You must be top dog, the 'pack leader' whose rules I follow. If you don't assume this position by teaching me to do what you say, I will try to usurp you and assume the pack leader position myself in an unspoken coup. If I feel like I am in charge I may well get increasingly anxious and proprietorial.

Dog training

Attending puppy socialization classes and dog training classes will help us both to develop a good relationship and will help you to teach me good manners and how to behave. Please remember that I do not speak your language; you will have to patiently teach me how to do what you want. I won't understand the words, but I will learn what you want me to when you make certain sounds. Learning appropriate hand signals will help me to further understand what you want. Training dogs is not difficult, but it requires time and patience from you. Two short, five-minute sessions daily will help me learn; if you put in the effort I will repay you by behaving beautifully (most of the time).

Basic commands

Keep training sessions short and please don't bother me with training if I have just had a meal, or if I am tired; all I will be interested in is sleeping and not learning. Pick the moment when I am likely to be at my most receptive. If I have just woken up and am doing high speed circuits of the garden, you might also find it hard to keep me focused.

Recall

This is the first lesson and a basic piece of obedience – you call, I come running. Some of us learn to come to our names quickly and easily, some are rather more wilful. Mostly this is not a problem with Frenchies as we like to stay close to our favourite humans.

When you're out for a walk with me, call my name and sound really excited. Just use my name, or the word 'come', not 'come here', or 'here'! When I respond, reward me with a treat and make a HUGE fuss of me. I'll learn really quickly.

Once I have grasped this you may want me to come to you and sit, before I am rewarded, see technique on page 40.

Russell

Owned by Matt and Sabrina | Lives in London | @russellrustles

Russell is boisterous and attention-seeking,
but a sweetheart at his core. He's a Frenchie
of contrasts, a lover of home comforts and the
outdoors. He'll be your best friend for a back
scratch and a snack.

It is very unlikely that I will ever run you ragged trying to catch me. You can look smugly on as other dog owners call fruitlessly for their pets while I, in contrast, remain devotedly by your side.

If I am proving to be very resistant to recall try not feeding me before a walk and keep those high-status treats to hand on the walk. This helps to reinforce the message that you are the source of all good things and coming to you brings real benefits.

Sit

Put a treat in your hand in a fist. Hold your hand over my nose and say 'sit'. Lift your hand slightly upwards and backwards – as I lift my nose up to follow the treat I will naturally drop my bottom and go into a sit. Praise me.

Once I have grasped this command, practise saying it with me beside you as well as in front of you.

Get me to sit before you give me my meals. As I become more disciplined you can make me wait to go to it until you give me the 'off you go' command.

Down

Start this training once I have begun to grasp the 'sit' command. For good results at the start, do this training where I can lie down comfortably, either on my bed or on a rug.

Get me to 'sit' and reward me. Put another treat in the palm of your hand, say 'down'. Then move your hand slowly towards the ground, edging it just out of reach as my nose follows your hand down. I will lower my front legs and with a bit of luck my hindquarters will follow. If I get up to try to reach the treat just pop me back in the sit position, give me a treat, then try 'down' again. It might take a few attempts before I figure out what you want me to do, but I will get there.

Once I am beginning to grasp this instruction you might like to introduce a hand signal to support it. With the treat in the palm of your hand extend your index finger and point it downwards. Take the treat to my nose and repeat the same process with your hand so that I lie down. Make a huge fuss of me every time I get this right.

When I have grasped the basic principle, start practising the command away from my bed. I am quite well upholstered and will happily lie down on command virtually anywhere.

Wait

The wait command teaches me to stay where I am until you tell me what to do next. I'll wait until you put my food bowl on the floor and not almost knock you over in my effort to get at the food. I'll wait at gates and doors while you go ahead of me.

To teach me 'wait' first tell me to 'sit', then take a step backwards, still facing me, holding your hand palm up, then call me to you. You'll probably have to do a lot of practice before I start waiting. Just keep up with short bursts of training and I'll get the message. Keep distances very small and gradually extend them as I am following the instruction reliably. It doesn't matter if I lie down instead of sitting, just so long as I stay put. In time you will be able to leave me sitting waiting while you walk a distance away and there I will remain until you call me.

Use 'wait' every time you feed me. Make me sit, then tell me to wait until my food bowl is on the floor. I will keep getting up and try to rush it, but just raise the bowl in the air, put me back in the sit position and tell me to 'wait' again. Do this at each mealtime to reinforce the command.

Stay

'Stay' training starts in a similar way to 'wait'. Put me in the sit position, take a step forward with your right foot, holding your hand behind you with the palm facing me. I will probably get up and follow. Put me back in the sit position and try again. Eventually you will be able to take a step forward and step back beside me without my moving.

Praise me effusively when I do as you have asked. Always try to walk off with your right foot leading for the stay command, this is a visual clue for me. It will be surprisingly difficult for you to maintain this small detail, but it is important, it sends me a clear signal that I am doing a stay exercise (you set off with your left foot instead when I am walking to heel – see below).

As with teaching the 'wait' command, extend the 'stay' distance a little at a

time. Keep repeating the word 'stay' slowly, clearly and firmly. Turn and face me before you return to me. As I get even better at obeying you, when you have gone as far away from me as you wish, turn, face me and wait for five seconds before returning; keep extending the time you wait at a distance, 10 seconds, 20 seconds and so on.

In time you will be able to leave me, return to me, walking around the rear of me with me remaining in the downward position. I will be watching you closely the whole time. Always praise me calmly and quietly while I am still in the down position. Then release me with the 'off you go' command.

Heel

Although I am a small dog, I am strong and powerful and will drag you along in my wake. This is a miserable experience for both of us, your arms will be pulled out of their sockets, and you won't feel like you are in control. I will be panting and choking in

frustration as I attempt to go where I want to, at the speed I want to.

You need me to learn to walk comfortably beside you, with a slack lead, until you can safely let me off the lead and I can wander where I will. The sooner you can do this the better, so start my training in your garden before I am even allowed outside for a walk.

Decide which side you want me to 'heel' to and stick to it. In competitive obedience training I should be on your left, and because I respond to visual clues you should always lead off with your left foot first to reinforce the message that we are walking to heel. Remember, you lead with your right foot when we are doing a stay exercise. From the start, these consistent visual clues help me to understand and differentiate what you want me to do. If you don't intend to show me, pick whichever side suits you best, left-handed people may naturally prefer to have their Frenchie 'heel' to their right side (if this suits you better just remember to consistently lead off with the alternate foot when you are teaching me the stay exercise).

If you are heeling to your left, hold the loop of the lead in your right hand and use your left hand to keep my head level with your legs. Ultimately you are trying to keep my nose to the side of your leg. This may be too much of a challenge for me to begin but with lovely smelling treats in your hand I should remain happily by your side.

Put high-status treats in your left pocket, then reach up with your left hand, get a few treats in your hand and hold them in your fist. Let your hand hang by your side so that I can smell the treats, then say 'heel'. I will nose your hand in an effort to get at the treat. At very regular intervals give me a treat to keep me encouraged. Keep repeating the word 'heel' over and over again while I am following your instruction.

Getting me to walk to heel will always be much easier on the way home when I am tired, although if I am fed after a walk I may be in a hurry to get home for this treat! You can also train me to 'heel' in the garden off the lead, but always have those treats to hand.

If I am being resistant to walking to heel, another technique you can employ is to keep changing direction without warning. This will throw me as I am expecting you to keep moving forwards. Every time I start pulling, change direction again. It doesn't make for the most productive walk in terms of distance (and you might feel a little silly when other humans see you), but it will reinforce the notion that although you are slower than me, I cannot always rely on you to plod along behind me. You are taking charge of our direction of travel.

You can also pop a squeaky toy in your pocket, you want to keep bringing my attention back to you so that my lead is slack.

Some training tools, such as a Halti or a Gentle Lead are not very comfortable for short-nosed breeds, so you will have to be very disciplined and persistent with your training.

Leave

This command is designed to make me give up something without a fuss. It can be a life-saver (quite literally) if I have made off with something dangerous such as a bar of chocolate absentmindedly left within my reach, a blister pack of painkillers I've filched from your handbag, or a cooked bone stolen as you clear up after lunch.

It can also have practical advantages; some Frenchies are very toy-focused and a ball or a Frisbee can be a handy way of wearing us out quickly if you are short of time. However, it won't work as a strategy if you throw the ball once and I flatly refuse to give it up.

Start training me young by gently trying to remove a toy from my mouth. Say 'leave' in a firm but kind voice. If I hang on to the toy don't pull – tug is a fun game in itself. Just produce another toy and make it seem more exciting than the one I am clutching in my jaw. Say 'leave' again and offer me the new toy. If I drop the old toy make a fuss of me and give me the new toy. Reinforce this message over and over again.

Overcoming negative behaviour

My character will determine how easy I am to train, but I am a Frenchie so we should get there in the end. Never punish me for bad behaviour, no matter how angry you are; reward me when I behave well. Frenchies are very sensitive to mood and they will be unhappy and frightened if you are angry with them.

Barking

As a general rule, French Bulldogs are not great barkers. They will bark when someone comes to the door, but quieten as soon as they are in. We don't make the greatest guard dogs but we are good at sounding an alert!

However, there are exceptions to every rule. If I go into energetic overdrive and bark repeatedly whenever someone comes to the door, shouting, or trying to hold me back by the collar when you open the door won't help resolve the issue. Don't give me treats to distract me, because this will reward the barking, instead say, 'quiet' gently but firmly. When I stop barking, reward me.

Obviously, this doesn't help when you have someone at the door, so if I am causing mayhem enlist a friend or neighbour to help. Get them to come to the door and make their presence known. When I start barking say 'quiet' and wait until I stop, however long it takes. When I stop, give me a treat. Get your friend to knock or ring again, and repeat. This will take a little time, but I will catch on. This exercise also works well if I bark at other dogs when I am walking on the lead. Stop walking, say 'quiet' and when I stop barking reward me. Remember, I only get the reward when I am quiet.

If I bark at you in the house to get your attention – I am stubborn and I can keep this up for a while – ignore me! It's annoying, but don't respond until I stop barking, then reward me straight away.

Separation anxiety

This can easily become an issue with French Bulldogs who are devoted to their favourite people. If I am wide-awake, bored and full of beans when you depart, I am more likely to be in a state of high anxiety. If instead you always take me for a good walk before leaving me, I may just settle down to sleep. After the walk, give me something I really like, such as a Kong filled with peanut butter or frozen meat, though if I am really anxious I may not eat it until

you return. Put some calming music on the radio and if you are going out in the evening leave a light on. You can also give me one of your old jumpers that smells deliciously of you.

Don't make a fuss of me before you depart, just be calm and quiet, and do the same when you return. I know this is hard because my welcome is so effusive, after all I love you wildly – who else is so demonstrably thrilled to see you when you have only been out for five minutes? However, if my behaviour is causing issues this will help me to understand that calm is good and that your going out and returning is no big deal.

Dogs read your movements, so we will know when you grab your coat, your bag and your keys that you are going out. If I react badly to this you can work on me by going through the process, leaving, but return just a few moments later. If you keep doing this I will not get as anxious because I won't be sure you are actually leaving. You want to promote a calm atmosphere. Ignore me when you leave, and for a few minutes when you return.

Honey and Blu

Owned by Sarah | Live in West Sussex | @honey_blu_ghost

Honey and Blu live active and healthy lifestyles
and are happiest exploring the great outdoors.

If the problem is severe, please take me to see a dog trainer, or dog behaviour specialist, they can really help us to achieve a peaceful and happy life together.

Aggression

We Frenchies are an easy-going bunch. We like, or can learn to like, most people, dogs and other creatures. However, things can go a bit awry if I am not properly socialized, or if I have a dominant personality, or indeed am being flooded with testosterone. Young male dogs have to get used to other dogs responding to them very differently as they grow into adulthood and there can be hiccups. If you suspect hormones are the problem, and you don't like the idea of neutering me unnecessarily, vets can chemically castrate a dog, which is effective for around a year, before you decide whether or not the snip is the solution!

If I bark and lunge at other dogs you need to divert my attention to you. When you see another dog coming, get a treat in your hand and distract me with the treat so that I focus on you, instead of obsessing about the advancing pooch. If I have been attacked or bitten by another dog this may also make me more inclined to be suspicious of other dogs; you will have to work on my socialization by building up my trust in other dogs and encouraging calm behaviour.

Ultimately you are responsible if I bite or attack another dog and you can be fined for not keeping me under proper control. We tend to avoid fights, but if we take another dog on we don't like to back down – it's that stubborn streak again. If you are struggling, please seek professional help, your vet is a good place to find contact details for dog behaviourists. If a placid and friendly Frenchie suddenly becomes aggressive take them to the vet, it may be indicative of an undiagnosed physical problem.

The real secret to dog training is to understand that it is not something you ever stop doing. You can train me to sit and lie down on command, to wait and to stay as instructed, but the one thing you can guarantee, if you don't keep up the training I won't keep behaving beautifully.

Resource guarding

While we Frenchies are loving dogs, we are quite bullish in temperament – stubborn, pig-headed, obstinate and bloody minded are all adjectives that can be applied to me. In the home this can come out as resource guarding; we can get very possessive over a particular toy, our food bowl, a particular chair and even act like our owner's bed is our own.

We might be perfectly sociable outside the home, but hate other people, or other dogs coming into our home. This behaviour can be quite startling when it occurs, the dog can stiffen, growl, raise its hackles and threaten to bite. All dogs are susceptible to resource guarding; it is a perfectly natural behaviour in the wild, but less tolerable in a domestic situation. You need to nip this behaviour in the bud but handle the situation very carefully.

Your Frenchie is merely trying to protect what he/she regards as a valuable resource, so try to see things from our point of view. If you try to snatch a precious toy away from me, or to take away my food bowl because I am growling if you come close, I will only guard it more closely next time. Do not get cross, this will only aggravate the situation. You are aiming to diffuse the situation to reinforce positive behaviour and make me feel less threatened.

If I am possessive over my food bowl make sure I am not disturbed while I am eating. When I have walked away after eating, pick up my food bowl so that I cannot obsess over it. Don't leave it on the ground.

If I am possessive over a particular toy don't try to take it away from me. However, when I am out of the way remove the offending toy and hide it for a while.

If I will only allow one person to sit on the sofa with me, get me a new dog bed and keep putting treats in it to make it attractive. Keep me off the sofa.

If I become possessive over your bed, shut the bedroom door and don't allow me in.

Ideally seek the guidance of an animal behaviourist who can advise you on what techniques to use.

Diet

I love you more than anything else in the world, though food comes a very close second.

Mealtimes are my favourite time of the day. I treat each meal as a race, even if I am an only dog. I will gobble up my food in seconds, barely tasting it. This is not good for me. Special food bowls are available from pet shops that make it harder for me to eat quickly. I have to work to access the food in these bowls, using my tongue to tease out every last bit, and this slows down the rate at which I eat and might also help reduce the frequency of my gaseous emissions!

I can become very focused on my mealtimes. I might nag you as mealtime approaches, complaining in my special yodelling style that you are late feeding me – a heinous crime in my book! Just ignore me, if you feed me early today because I nag, I'll only push for my mealtime to be earlier again tomorrow.

If you are using a lot of treats in training, remember to deduct the overall amount from my meal allowance. This way my treats are just part of my daily rations. Once I have grasped the basics, you can try rewarding my good behaviour with methods that won't add inches to my waistline.

Weight

Frenchies are small but well-muscled dogs. We are not a bony breed and with our healthy appetites it is easy for us to gain weight. If I am only fed at mealtimes and I get one hour of exercise a day, my weight should not become a problem.

Male Frenchies should weigh no more than 12.5kg (28lb) and females no more than 11kg (24lb). However, this is not a hard and fast rule; some dogs have a bigger build, and some are small for the breed. Our stature may be solid and muscular, but we should still have a waist and although you shouldn't be able to see our ribs, you should just be able to feel them if you run your hands along our sides.

As with you humans, carrying extra weight can lead to other health problems, including diabetes and hip dysplasia, plus it can make breathing harder for us, very undesirable in a breed that suffers from respiratory disorders. A high-fibre, low-fat, complete food diet, with fewer calories per kilo, can be utilized to help me shed some pounds. I won't feel cheated if

Don't give me any of these foods:

Alcohol isn't much good for humans, it's not good for Frenchies either. As well as all the obvious symptoms of alcohol poisoning (sickness and diarrhoea), it can also damage my central nervous system.

Avocado contains persin, a fungicidal toxin that is harmless to humans, but which can cause vomiting and diarrhoea in dogs. It is present in the seed, the fruit, the skin and the leaves.

Caffeine is not good for dogs. If we consume excessive amounts, it can have a similar effect to chocolate. Don't give us coffee or tea.

Chocolate contains a compound called theobromine; it is fine for humans, who can process it, but it can kill all dogs, even in small amounts. If I have eaten chocolate call the vet straight away and ask their advice. Note how much chocolate has been consumed and whether it is dark or milk chocolate, as your vet will want to know; dark chocolate contains more theobromine. Depending on how much chocolate has been consumed the vet may want to make me vomit, and they may administer charcoal to absorb the poison.

Cooked bones are highly dangerous. They can splinter and damage my internal organs, often causing perforation of the gut. Raw bones are safe, but only give me a large raw bone, small ones can cause choking.

Corn-on-the-cob is not poisonous to dogs, but it can cause a blockage in a dog's intestine and be potentially fatal.

Grapes, sultanas and raisins can cause liver damage and kidney failure in some dogs. It is impossible to predict whether or not we might be affected, so do not give us grapes, sultanas or raisins, and please think twice before you offer me a morsel of that carrot cake or fruit cake!

Macadamia nuts are toxic to dogs; they can cause severe pain, muscle tremors and limb paralysis.

Onions, garlic and chives, indeed anything from the onion family, is toxic to dogs and can cause serious gastrointestinal irritation and red blood cell damage.

Xylitol is an artificial sweetener used in many low-fat and diet products, but it is highly toxic to all dogs, including Frenchies. It can induce hypoglycaemia (low blood sugar) and is linked to liver failure and blood clotting disorders.

you feed me this, or you can just cut back on portions of my regular food. If you can help get me back into shape I will enjoy exercise more and that will in turn help maintain my proper figure.

All dogs are omnivores, eating both plant and animal matter to survive. However, we cannot eat anything and everything.

Nutrition

There is an enormous array of commercial dog food on the market and, as with human food, there are an increasing number of specialist products on offer – wheat intolerance, gluten intolerance, hypo-allergenic, vegan and sensitive tummies are all catered for. You can feed us a purely dry diet, a mix of wet and dry, cook your own meals as you might for a baby, get freshly cooked frozen meals delivered to your door, or follow the unfortunately named BARF (Biologically Appropriate Raw Food) diet.

If you study the labels, you will find it hard to make direct comparisons of the nutrient content between the different forms of dog food. Protein and fat are important components, as are a good balance of vitamins and minerals. We Frenchies need different quantities of nutrients at different stages of our lives; puppies have a much higher protein diet and the requirements of senior dogs (7+ years) are different again to that of a lively adult French Bulldog.

High-quality foods generally contain less in the way of fillers and more nutritional ingredients, cheaper foods will use more fillers to satisfy appetite.

Most adult dog foods contain around 20–30 per cent protein (5–8 per cent in wet foods) and 9–14 per cent fat (2–4 per cent in wet foods). Dietary fibre (vegetable matter) maintains intestinal health and helps to treat both constipation and diarrhoea and has a probiotic function. Ash is a measure of the mineral content of food, and includes calcium, copper, iron, magnesium, manganese, phosphorus, potassium, selenium and zinc. There are 13 vitamins that are important for health; vitamin A, vitamin C, vitamin D, vitamin E, vitamin K and eight B vitamins.

Protein usually comes in the form of meat and fish, but vegetables can also supply proteins and these protein sources are cheaper. Protein from non-meat sources such as soya, maize and potato, are harder for the dog to digest and can in some instances cause dietary intolerance. Raw meat BARF diets have a much higher protein content and, as the meat is uncooked, it retains its nutrients. The nature of the protein content in dog food can vary from pure meat, to rendered meat meal, bone or animal derivatives.

Fats and oils are important for a Frenchie's skin and fur and are also a good source of energy. Some essential fatty acids, such as omega-3, which is also important for health, are often added to commercial dog food.

Fillers make up the remaining percentage of dog food. This is likely to include whole grains such as wheat, barley, corn, rice, oats, rye and sorghum, many of which also include important nutrients. It may also include peas, potatoes, sweet potatoes, quinoa and lentils, which are higher in calories.

As with all food purchases, you get what you pay for, but I may well be perfectly happy and thrive with a

competitively priced dog food. If you are concerned about quality don't rely on the front of the packaging for information, look at the ingredients listed on the back. If I am thriving, everything is fine, but if I start getting tummy upsets or skin conditions you may have to pay more careful attention to my diet.

Always be guided by your vet, dogs are less likely to develop food allergies than humans – they have robust digestive systems – but allergies to surroundings are more common irritants. Anecdotal evidence suggests that Frenchies may be more prone to food allergies than some other dog breeds, but seek professional advice if we are getting skin disorders or runny poo on a regular basis, don't assume we have a food allergy. Simply changing food brands will do nothing, I will be allergic to an ingredient and not a brand, and you will need help identifying what the cause might be.

Complete food, a specially formulated diet in the form of kibble, is perhaps the simplest way to ensure that I get a nutritionally balanced diet. If it is kept in

Zelma

Owned by Lindha | Lives in Sweden | @zelmathefrenchie

Zelma is smart, intelligent and social. She is a
service dog so always joins us on travels and has
friends and fans all over the world.

an air-tight container it has a good shelf life.

Wet meat food, in the form of tins or pouches, is usually served with biscuits or kibble to ensure all the nutritional requirements are met.

The BARF diet imitates the diet a dog would have in the wild and is high in protein. It consists of 60–75 per cent raw meat and bones, which can be in the form of chicken wings and necks, or raw fish. The remainder consists of fruit and vegetables, offal, eggs or dairy food and is made up by you to create the nutritional whole. To make life simpler manufacturers now sell the meaty part of this diet, which is delivered frozen, and portions can then be defrosted as required. You have to be quite committed to put me on this diet, it's not cheap and requires a lot of proactive food preparation from you. If you choose to feed me the BARF diet, please follow all the usual hygiene precautions in handling raw meat.

In many countries around the world you can also buy specially prepared, nutritionally appropriate, cooked meals online, which are then delivered frozen to your door. This is a premium product. I will love it, but it doesn't come cheap.

Wind

Pardon me! One of the reasons that Frenchies may be prone to wind is that we gobble our food up so quickly. If I am frequently contaminating your air space with noxious fumes, first try feeding me twice a day and buy a bowl designed to make me eat more slowly. If you think a food intolerance could be the problem, consult your vet as to the best course of action. Low-fibre diets that contain less in the way of soya, beans and peas may help, and probiotic powders can be prescribed. However, when all is said and done, there is probably not a Frenchie owner alive who won't admit that regular gaseous emissions are a noisy and fragrant feature of their beloved dog's day-to-day life!

Water

Please make sure I always have water available and wash my water bowl daily, it really isn't good for me to drink stale and dirty water – even though I may well drink happily from a muddy puddle out on a walk. Please keep some water in the car for me and a travelling water bowl so that you can always offer me a drink. I often badly need some refreshing water at the end of a walk.

Doggy ice cream

As a flat-faced breed my respiratory system is challenged, and it is hard for me to cool down when it is hot. A doggy ice cream or doggy ice pop is a very welcome treat when it is hot as it will help cool down my internal temperature. Please don't give me human ice cream – it's not good for me – but specially made doggy versions are fine. These often contain plain yoghurt (authentic Greek yoghurt or goat's milk yoghurt is easier for me to digest) or coconut milk and oil, combined with peanut butter and banana. If you make your own doggy ice cream, please make sure your peanut butter does not contain the artificial sweetener xylitol, which is dangerous for dogs. Remember to keep the portion size Frenchie appropriate, we are only small!

Frenchie Fact

- **The daughter of Tsar** Nicholas II, Tatiana Romanov (1897–1918), had a model of her French Bulldog Ortipo immortalized in hardstone by Fabergé. After its death Tatiana acquired Ortipo II, who went into exile with her, and is thought to have met the same tragic fate as his owner at the hands of the Bolsheviks in 1918. Fabergé's likeness of the dog can still be seen at the Kremlin Museum in Moscow.

Grooming

Brushing and cleaning

We Frenchies have short, fine, soft coats where the whorls of our fur can be seen clearly. We don't need daily brushing to keep our coats in good condition, as some longer-haired breeds require, but very regular grooming is still enormously important for us.

We like to be clean and it helps keep us healthy, so do your best to make our grooming ritual pleasant right from the start so that this regular maintenance programme is always a pleasure and never a chore.

I have very sensitive skin and keeping me clean helps me avoid skin issues. All those cute folds and wrinkles harbour dust, dirt, bits of food, dander and clumps of hair. In this warm and damp environment, it is easy for bacteria and yeast to go forth and multiply, which will cause all kinds of skin irritations. Ideally, you will clean our crevices every two to three days as a minimum. If you do so, these problems are far less likely to occur, plus it keeps me smelling clean fresh. You can use an anti-bacterial baby wipe, or just a moistened cotton wool ball, to remove all the gunk. Dry my folds to remove any traces of moisture.

Brace yourselves, it's not just the folds that can use a wipe over every few

Frenchie Fact

- **Two of Lady Gaga's three** French Bulldogs, Koji and Gustav, were stolen at gunpoint in Los Angeles in February 2021. A friend who was walking the dogs was shot in the robbery, though made a full recovery. The dogs were handed in two days later and reunited with their owner. A man is now serving a jail sentence for their theft.

days, it is our bottoms. We have short, muscular tails that tend to naturally cover our bottom, and we often have a generous fold or pocket below the tail, but above the bottom, in which 'matter' can accumulate. This is more of a problem for some Frenchies than others, however, it does mean that when we poo, there is not always a perfectly clean drop. Apologies, there really is no delicate way of putting it. While most breeds of dogs can competently clean their own bottoms, we Frenchies just can't reach round that far. Therefore, all you kind and doting Frenchie owners will need to give us some assistance! Please wipe all around our bottoms with an anti-bacterial wipe every couple of days as an absolute minimum and wipe the folds and pouches in the area to avoid any bacterial build-up!

Much less offensive is the issue of tear staining. A number of dog breeds are susceptible to this issue, especially those that are categorized as brachycephalic or flat-faced breeds. The red/brown staining is caused by porphyrin pigment – iron-containing molecules – excreted via a dog's tears, saliva and urine. The problem is more noticeable in pale-coloured breeds. Clean the area every other day with a soft, damp cloth or pad. Please just use warm water, you don't want to use anything stronger near the eye, and then dry the area to discourage bacteria. Tear staining is perfectly normal and not indicative of a health problem, but if we start pawing at our eyes repeatedly, please take us to the

vet as it may indicate a separate eye problem.

Regular grooming will help us to keep ourselves clean and healthy and, if you use the right equipment, we will enjoy the experience. Regular brushing stimulates blood circulation and spreads my natural oils through my coat, which should help ensure I look at my glossiest best. This is also a good opportunity for you to give me the once over and make sure I am healthy with no unexplained lumps and bumps. Use a rubber grooming mitt, which gently removes dead hair, or a soft bristle brush.

Bathing

Frenchies tend not to be natural water lovers, which doesn't make bathing the happiest of experiences. Please remember that we have good reason to be nervous of the water – we have very large, heavy heads which makes swimming difficult. We are naturally top-heavy. If you are taking me out on the water, please equip me with a life jacket; if there is an accidental spill I will struggle to stay afloat.

If you need to bathe me, wet me thoroughly, completely avoiding my face and ears, then apply a dog shampoo for sensitive skin – a human shampoo can give me skin irritation. My skin really is prone to upsets so please take care what dog shampoo you use. Give me a good rub all over to clean my fur then rinse me gently, making sure you remove all traces of the shampoo, as any residue will cause irritation. Please avoid getting any water in my ears – it might trigger an ear infection. Clean my face separately with a clean cloth dipped in warm water then wrung out. For more detailed instructions on how to look after my large, soft ears, see Health and First Aid.

Once I am clean, have lots of warm towels to hand. Put one on the floor, put me on to it, then put another towel on top of me. Rub me briskly, I will enjoy this. It is very important that you dry me thoroughly as the warm and moist environment of my folds and wrinkles will breed bacterial and yeast infections if not kept clean and dry. You can also give me a good brush with a dry bristle brush as this will also help remove any traces of water at the roots of my fur.

As further insurance against problems, take a small, soft brush, a paintbrush can be utilized here, dip it in baby powder and tickle the brush around my folds. Baby powder will help absorb any residual moisture.

Smile please

You can help to keep my teeth clean by giving me raw bones to chew, or you can get specially designed chews that are supposed to help prevent the build-up of plaque and tartar. Feeding me with dry food and hard dog biscuits is also helpful.

If I develop bad breath this may indicate gum disease and a serious build-up of tartar will require the vet to give my teeth a deep clean. This has to be done under anaesthetic; it's an unnecessary expense for you and I certainly won't enjoy the experience. What's more, neglecting my teeth can lead to the development of other serious health problems.

You can also clean my teeth every couple of days. I know it sounds crazy! Use special doggy toothpaste, which tastes of meat, so I don't mind

the experience. Do not use human toothpaste on me, it can be harmful. Gently rub the toothpaste over my teeth; get me used to this experience by simply rubbing a little bit of doggy toothpaste over a couple of teeth, nothing more. Gradually increase the amounts of toothpaste and time spent on the task over a week or so. Get me used to you manipulating my lips so that you can reach all areas of my teeth; either use a small toothbrush or a specially designed finger-brush – which slips over your finger – to clean my teeth. Give me plenty of treats to reward me for standing still and cooperating.

Ear, ear

If you keep my ears clean it will help me to avoid ear infections. Every couple of weeks dip a cotton wool ball in warm water, squeeze it out so it is damp – not dripping – and gently wipe the inside of my ears. Never use a cotton bud on me, you are likely to do more damage than good. Dry my ear gently with a tissue or soft cloth.

Pedicure

My nails grow like yours and shouldn't be allowed to get too long. Pavement walking helps to keep them in shape, but you will still need to trim my nails. Get someone to show you how to perform this task before trying it at home. If you are not confident leave nail-trimming to the professionals.

My nail contains the quick; the vessel that brings blood to the nail. If you cut my nail too short you will cut this, it will be painful and I will bleed. I will also not want you to come anywhere near my nails again.

If you can hear my nails click-clacking when I walk across a hard floor it is a sign that my nails are too long. Long, uncut nails can lead to lameness.

Trimming little and often is the best policy for pedicures. If you trim my nails every two weeks, you will only need to take off a small piece of the nail. I will be suspicious of this process initially but in time I will relax and behave while you give me my pedicure. You will become more confident in performing this procedure and can dare to cut a little closer to the quick.

When you are giving me a pedicure and have a hold of my paw, take the opportunity to examine my pads and my webbed toes to make sure everything is in good shape.

Frenchie Fact

- **The British monarch** Edward VII (1841–1910) had a French Bulldog named Peter. His wife, Queen Alexandra, also had a Frenchie named Paul who was immortalized in an ivory miniature.

Tiny
Companions

All animals accommodate a host of tiny friends and although my coat is short, there are still plenty of places for all kinds of things to hide – I have lots of crevices and folds that small things can creep into!

Fleas

As sure as night follows day I will get fleas. Fleas are everywhere; cats and humans shouldn't get too high and mighty about them, because you have your own cat fleas and human fleas too. I can pick them up from another dog, a cat, your home, your friend's home, or from your clothes or your shoes.

These tiny parasites are superb jumpers, which is how they hop from their environment, to host, to home, to host and so on. Females must have a meal of blood before they lay eggs; up to 50 eggs per day. The eggs are like tiny grains of sand, they fall off me when they are laid, then hatch into larvae within two to five days. The larvae, which are around 5mm (¼in) long, live in carpets, soft furnishings and cracks in the floorboards. They feed and after around two weeks build a cocoon, from which they pupate as adult fleas when a food source is

nearby. The entire life cycle takes around three to four weeks. Fleas can also pass tapeworm on to me, see more information below.

Fleas are particularly active when the weather is warmer, but they can still reproduce inside the home in winter. Moreover, fleas can lie dormant in a home for a long time when there is no food source, but the arrival of a pet stimulates them to hatch. If you are moving house, make sure my flea treatments are up to date.

Dog fleas prefer dogs, cat fleas prefer cats, but they will hop on any host in extremis, even you! If you are getting bitten by fleas it suggests that our home has a serious flea problem.

If I have fleas, bear in mind that only approximately 5 per cent of the flea population will be on me, the remaining 95 per cent will be in our home! Spot-on treatments only kill the adult fleas, so if there is an infestation it can take up to three months to eradicate the problem. The best solution is to consistently use appropriate preventative flea treatments from the moment I come into your life as a puppy.

Puppies require specific flea treatments suitable for their age and weight; the earliest this can be administered is usually at eight weeks. Some treatments are not suitable for young puppies so always consult your vet. Fleas can trouble puppies badly, they can have an adverse reaction to flea bites, leading to allergic dermatitis, and in severe infestations a puppy can develop life-threatening anaemia.

How can you tell if I have fleas? Scratching is a tell-tale sign, but you can see evidence of fleas too; part my coat at the back of my neck, or near my ears, or at the base of my tail and look for tiny black specks that look like pepper. This is flea dirt, basically digested blood and very unsavoury. If you put this on a piece of paper and dampen it, it will turn red and you have your proof that I have fleas.

Chemical spot-on treatments, which are administered to the back of the neck and between the shoulder blades, are very effective. These will also render all the flea eggs infertile. Live fleas will be killed within 24 hours and some flea treatments also kill ticks.

Please remember to wash my pet bedding regularly, hoover floors thoroughly and don't forget the soft furnishings. Empty the contents of the dustbag after hoovering!

If you follow this regime fleas should never become a problem. However, if you do let things slide and your house has a serious flea infestation – you will probably be being bitten too at this point – you will also need to use a chemical spray treatment on your house to help kill the pesky things.

Ticks

Like fleas, ticks will climb on to me when I am out on a walk, then enjoy a drink of my blood. The tick will stay in place until it has had enough to drink, when it will drop off. Ticks can cause severe skin irritation and can also transmit Lyme disease, borreliosis, which is a tick-transmitted bacterial infection that is found in Europe, North America and Asia, and which can affect you humans as well as me.

Ticks are very common in areas where there is wildlife or livestock and are most commonly seen in warmer weather. They start off very small, but grow as they feed; you can see these or feel them on me, my short coat usually ensures they are spotted quite quickly.

Ticks resemble a skin tag and can be light in colour, or grey, or quite dark. The part you can see is the tick's large, flat body. Don't attempt to pull it straight off me, this can result in cross contamination as parts of the mouth can remain in situ.

Ticks are easily removed with a tick tool which allows you to anchor the body while you then twist the tool. This effectively unscrews the tick from its food source. Once you have removed the tick, squash it very hard between some paper and dispose of the body. It is best to purchase a tick tool when you get a puppy, then you always have it to hand when needed; it's cheap to buy. You can buy a tick tool from most pet shops. Vaccinations against Lyme disease are now available if you are concerned that I am at high risk.

If you are worried that I have contracted Lyme disease from a tick, take me to the vet.

Honey

Owned by Andrew and Matthew | Lives in Manchester | @honeyandted

Honey is a happy and goofy little Frenchie who
loves giving kisses and being the centre
of attention!

Worms

Dogs can and will pick up worms from numerous sources: soil, vegetation or faeces can be contaminated with worm eggs and contaminated fleas can pass tapeworm to your dog. Worms can be passed from dog to dog via their faeces, and though it is unusual, it can also be passed on to you. It's another good reason for all dog owners to scoop that poop!

Worms can cause diarrhoea and vomiting, weight loss, weakness, coughing and anaemia. Puppies with worms get an abnormally swollen tummy. If you see me scooting – dragging my bottom along the floor – it is an indication that I might have worms, though I can do this for other reasons too, so get me checked out by the vet.

Intestinal worms

Roundworms are passed on to a puppy via its mother's milk and adult dogs can contract them from contaminated soil or meat. These look like spaghetti in my poo, but spaghetti that wriggles around!

Hookworms and whipworms live in my intestines where they latch on with sharp teeth to suck my blood. Weight loss is a common symptom and I contract them via contaminated soil.

Tapeworms are spread by infected fleas. They can also be spotted around my anus and look like grains of rice in my poo. I pick them up if I accidentally ingest an infected flea while grooming myself. As the flea is digested the tapeworm egg is released and hatches, whereupon it latches on to my small intestine. Occasionally an entire tapeworm can be passed or vomited up – not a pleasant experience for anyone, so keep on top of my flea control!

All dogs should be regularly wormed, and there are numerous deworming medications available. Puppies are at particular risk from worms but please seek advice from your vet before worming your puppy.

Lungworm

Lungworm, *Angiostrongylus vasorum*, is fairly common in some countries and it can kill. I can contract it if I consume its larvae, which are found in infected slugs, snails and frogs. Dogs can accidentally eat small slugs if they are on their toys or their fur. The lungworm moves through the dog's body and finally settles in the heart and blood vessels. We excrete the larvae in our poo, this infects more slugs and snails, which can then in turn infect more dogs.

Symptoms include:

- Coughing
- Breathing problems
- Reluctance to exercise
- Abnormal blood clotting

Take me to the vet if I am displaying any of these symptoms; the vet will need to prescribe a special course of medication to eliminate lungworm. In some areas where lungworm is especially prevalent it is advisable to give me preventative medication.

Heartworm

The dirofilariasis parasite is transmitted via the bite of an infected mosquito and affects dogs, cats and ferrets. It is found in large swathes of the USA and Canada but is rarely seen in the UK. There are 30 species of mosquito that transmit it. Heartworm kills dogs, but as it takes several years before symptoms appear, the disease is often well advanced by the time clinical signs are visible. Blood tests can confirm a diagnosis and X-rays will show the extent of the damage. Medication is given via a series of injections. It is critical that dogs are kept quiet during treatment and for several months afterwards, never easy for a young lively Frenchie. If you live in areas where heartworm can be contracted, preventive medication is recommended.

Symptoms include:

- Dry cough
- Shortness of breath
- Listlessness
- Loss of stamina

Mites

Ear mites, *Otodectes cynotis*, are common in cats, but can affect dogs as well, so if your dog has ear mites always check their feline friends too. The parasites live in the outer ear canal. Symptoms include ear scratching and shaking of the head so that the ears flap. The ear will become red and inflamed and you may see a waxy brown discharge. Untreated ear mites can lead to other ear infections. The ear will need to be regularly cleaned and treated with medicated ear drops prescribed by the vet. Regular flea treatment should act as a preventative.

Fur mites, *Cheyletiella*, commonly dubbed 'walking dandruff', are a common canine mite. This small, white mite lives on the surface of the skin and causes mild itchiness; one of the obvious signs of a fur mite infestation is a coat full of small flakes of skin, or scurf.

Harvest mites, *Neotrombicula autumnalis*, are small, bright orange mites that can also affect cats and humans. They can easily be picked up in grassy areas or woodland in late summer and autumn. This mite causes intense itching and inflammation in the feet and lower leg, as well as scabs and pus, but it can also affect the armpits, the tummy and the genitals and very occasionally the ears. It can be seen with the naked eye. It is easily treated with an insecticide and anti-inflammatories may be required to ease discomfort. Regular flea treatments should deal with this problem without it ever becoming an issue.

Mange

There are two types of skin mites that can cause mange: *Demodex canis*, and *Sarcoptes scabiei*. A dog with a good immune system should not fall prey to demodectic mange, but puppies can be at risk as they cannot stop the parasite, and it is usually passed from mother to pup. The parasite lives within hair follicles and causes the skin to become very itchy; hair loss and lesions can develop. It spreads from the point of infection and across the whole body, the dog's skin appears to turn a blue/grey. You won't be able to see these parasites with the naked eye, they can only be seen through a microscope.

This form of mange does not easily spread to other dogs or to humans and is treated with a topical preparation.

Scabies, however, is highly contagious. I don't have to come into direct contact with another creature to catch it and it can be passed on to humans. All dogs in the household will need to be treated with a medicated shampoo. Foxes are a common source of contagion.

Frenchie Fact

- **French Bulldogs** can make good therapy dogs. They pick up on the moods and emotions of the people around them, are quiet, affectionate and, as they crave attention, enjoy being petted.

Health and First Aid

Obesity is one of the biggest threats to the health of a French Bulldog. Don't show your love by giving me excess treats, it is not a kindness.

If you stick to this rule, use treats for training purposes only and give me sufficient exercise – an hour a day is enough – you should have a happy, healthy French Bulldog. I have a robust, well-muscled physique and a short coat. My eyes should be bright, my nose damp and my coat kept clean and fresh. I tend to overheat in warm weather, see below, but in winter I am grateful for some extra protection. Although I look well-built,

I am not good at keeping myself warm when it is cold, and if neglected can suffer from hypothermia. Depending on your local winter temperatures I may need a fleece or a waterproof padded jacket to stop my temperature dropping too low. I hate the rain, so a waterproof coat helps me cope with the wet.

The development of my breed to produce our short, flat noses and big eyes has left us prone to a number of genetic conditions. Breeders are now actively attempting to reduce these problematic conditions by only putting the healthiest dogs to stud and by use of genetic testing for some

conditions. If you have purchased me from a reputable breeder, my chance of suffering is considerably reduced.

French Bulldogs are classed as brachycephalic; 'brachy' means 'shortened' and 'cephalic' means 'head'. Other dogs in this group include pugs, King Charles Spaniels, English Bulldogs, Shih Tzus and Pekingese. You can find more information on these conditions and other disorders further on in this chapter. However, you would be advised to take out health insurance for me, as some of these problems are very expensive to treat.

Pills and medicine

Please don't ever give me any form of human medicine unless my vet specifically suggests it and advises the dosage.

Prescribed liquid medication is fairly easy to administer if you have a little doggy medicine syringe – nine times out of ten this comes with the medicine.

Pills can be more of a challenge. You can try holding my body gently between your legs, get the pill in one hand and with the other lift my head upwards and

The French Bulldog is classified as Category 2 in the Kennel Club Breed Watch programme and it highlights the following concerns:

- Dogs showing respiratory distress, including difficulty breathing or laboured breathing
- Exaggerated roach (rise) in the top line which should be level
- Hair loss or scarring from previous dermatitis
- Incorrect bite
- Lack of tail, screw tail, inverted tail and tight tail
- Pinched nostrils
- Prominent eyes
- Short neck
- Signs of dermatitis in skin folds

open my mouth. You want to drop the pill towards the back of my throat. Hold my jaws closed and stroke my throat to encourage me to swallow.

First aid kit

As with you humans, accidents occur, and if one does it is helpful to have a first aid kit to hand, which should include:

- Antiseptic wipes
- Pressurized saline wound wash
- Dog antiseptic cream
- Sterile gauze dressings
- Self-adhesive bandage
- A dog boot, in case of cut or injured paws

Cuts

We safety-conscious Frenchies have a short but dense coat and tend not to live dangerously, preferring to trot along close to our owners. However, any dog can have an accident. If I injure myself it may look worse than it is. The first thing to do is to get me to sit down to slow my heartbeat. This will allow you to assess the severity of the injury. Apply gentle pressure to the cut.

If you are unsure, please contact my vet straight away for advice. If stitches are required, the sooner it is done the better, although I will be ungrateful and won't thank you. The vet will have to anaesthetize me, not straightforward with Frenchies, and may need to keep me in overnight. I will be very wobbly after an anaesthetic, so please carry me into the house. Help me on to my bed or on to the sofa so I can be close to you. I will sleep.

I will also need the 'cone of shame' (buster collar), or a medical pet shirt, because I must not be allowed to worry at my stitches. The collar can come off on walks and for meals – I will be able to access my water bowl with it on, no matter what I would have you believe.

If my foot has been injured you may have to cover it with a plastic shoe so that the dressing doesn't get wet – even in summer; the grass is covered with dew in the morning.

I will be on lead walks for a minimum of ten days, the vet will guide you. They will want to give me regular check-ups to ensure that everything is healing as it should, and any dressings will need to be regularly changed.

Heat exhaustion

All dog owners should be aware not to leave us in cars in full sun or even in the shade when it is hot, but this is doubly true for French Bulldogs. My breed, along with all brachycephalic breeds, cannot cool ourselves down by panting as effectively as other breeds and we can overheat and die very quickly. Even if it doesn't feel that warm, a car, a caravan or a conservatory can heat up very quickly. When it is 22°C (72°F) outside, the interior temperature of a car can quickly rise to 47°C (117°F). To keep us safe, it is best not to leave us in the car alone at all, not ever!

On a hot day Frenchies really enjoy a doggy ice cream or ice lolly which can help lower their internal body temperature. Ice cubes in our water bowl have a similar effect.

We can also get heat exhaustion on a summer walk if you allow us to run too much. Ball fanatics won't stop chasing after a ball you are throwing for us because we are getting too hot. If there is no water nearby, we will have no way of cooling down and as a top-heavy Frenchie the chances are I won't want to fling myself into a pond to cool down – I might drown!

If I show any of the following symptoms, then I have dangerously overheated:

- Panting rapidly
- Making an unusual sound
- Producing foamy saliva
- Vomiting
- Red and floppy tongue
- Disorientated, confused or swaying

First, cool me down. Wet a large towel with cool, not cold water and place it over me. Put a fan on me or gently sprinkler water over the towel every so often – a watering can with a sprinkle head on will do the job perfectly. Overheating to this extent can cause long term damage and I should be checked out by the vet. It can take me some days to recover.

If the weather is hot, exercise me first thing in the morning, or late in the evening when it is cooler. Keep me indoors in the shade where I can stay cool. If you live in a warm climate I will need air conditioning, or a fan as a minimum to help me cope.

Diarrhoea

If the world is falling out of my bottom, the chances are that either you have made an alteration to my diet, which may not suit me, or, and this is the likelier of the two, I have scavenged something to eat that has not agreed with me.

The first course of action is to withhold food for a day, but make sure I have water on hand, as diarrhoea can lead to dehydration. After 24 hours feed me something bland; cooked chicken or white fish with boiled rice is ideal. Give me a small portion and allow me plenty of time to digest it before giving me more. This will usually sort everything out. However, if things don't improve please take me to the vet.

If you see blood in my faeces, or if I am vomiting as well, call the vet.

Vomiting

I will vomit sometimes, like all dogs. It may be that I have gobbled my food too quickly. If this happens you will probably be horrified to see me happily tucking in to eat the whole splatted mess all over again. Greedy puppies are especially prone to this, so if it happens regularly, feed me the same amount but split it into smaller portions more times a day and use a slow feeding bowl. Don't let me tear around straight after eating.

I quite like to eat grass, but I may vomit after eating it; don't worry about this.

If I vomit repeatedly, I may have eaten something unpleasant. Follow the same principle of withholding food for 24 hours then feeding a bland diet, as with diarrhoea above.

If I am vomiting frequently, or if you notice something resembling blood, or faecal matter – and smelling really foul – take me straight to the vet.

Coughing

A very occasional cough is nothing to worry about, but a regular cough should be checked out by my vet. Kennel cough is an airborne disease, usually a virus, that easily spreads between dogs. I can be inoculated annually against kennel cough and the vaccination will lower my chances of catching it and reduce my symptoms if I do. Most boarding

Sunny

Owned by Jolanta and Remi | Lives in Newcastle, UK | @sunny.french

A lover of kisses, cuddles and long morning
naps in the sun. Sunny loves to play and makes
everyone laugh.

kennels insist that I am inoculated against kennel cough before a stay. If am not vaccinated, I can pick up kennel cough from infected dogs. Most dogs with kennel cough aren't too poorly, but some of us can be badly affected and may need anti-inflammatories to bring down our temperature and reduce inflammation in our airways. If I am lethargic, refuse to eat or develop breathing problems take me straight to the vet.

You will need to keep me away from other dogs for two to three weeks after my symptoms have disappeared. Don't let me race around if I have kennel cough as this can make symptoms worse; give me gentle exercise on a lead.

A cough can also be indicative of heart disease, especially if it happens after exercise or in the evening. Ask a vet to listen to my heart to make sure that this isn't the cause of the coughing.

Ears

My distinctive ears are described as bat-shaped; they sit high on my head and stand erect, though they might flop when I am a puppy. The upright shape is good for ear health as it allows air circulation. Keep my ears clean please and check them regularly – see the chapter on grooming.

Dogs with floppy ears are more likely to suffer from ear infections. However, my ear canals are narrow so bacteria and yeast can flourish here. Plus, because my ears stand erect, dirt and fluff can get caught in them.

If my ears are red, hot to the touch, are itchy – I keep rubbing them – and have an unpleasant smell, I might have an ear infection. Please take me to see the vet, I might need drops, ointment or antibiotics. Over-the-counter products are not recommended, please consult an expert.

If I start scratching my ear or shaking my head, have a look inside, there may be a grass seed, a burr, or some other foreign body that is causing discomfort. If you can see something obvious remove it gently – damp cotton wool is good for this. Don't probe into the ear or use ear buds. If the foreign body doesn't lift out easily, I will need a trip to the vet.

If you can see a dark discharge in the ear that looks like coffee grounds, I may have ear mites; see the chapter on tiny companions.

Skin irritation

Skin allergies can have a number of trigger factors: oversensitivity can be caused by fleas (see the tiny companions chapter), pollen, grass, moulds, house-dust mites and some foods. The skin becomes itchy, red and can be hot to the touch. Bald patches and skin infections can develop. The bad news is that Frenchies seem to be susceptible to dermatitis. Our skin folds can lead to a build-up of bacteria or yeast, both of which can upset my skin. It is essential you practice a thorough and regular grooming regime (please see the chapter on grooming). Please make an appointment for me to see the vet if you are concerned; skin problems tend to get worse if they are left untreated. They will help you to determine what are my trigger factors (please see the chapter on diet).

Bites and stings

If you own a dog, any dog, the chances are that at some point they will become involved in some nose-to-nose power posturing. We Frenchies generally don't look for trouble, but if we decide to engage in a fight we won't want to back down. If we do get bitten you should get us checked out.

Wasps and bees

Frenchies, just like you humans, will suffer irritation if we are stung by wasps and bees. First, check to make sure that the sting itself is not still stuck in me; if it is, remove it carefully, scraping it out rather than pulling it out as this can release more venom. Bathe the area with cool water to help reduce the swelling. Most dogs suffer minor pain and irritation, however, if the area is swelling rapidly, or if I am having difficulty breathing or vomiting, take me straight to the emergency vet.

Snake bites

Snake bites can be fatal. In the UK it is only the adder that can cause we Frenchies serious harm, but in countries such as America and Australia, there are far more venomous snakes that can strike. If you see me worrying

something in the grass call me to you immediately.

The majority of snake bites occur in the spring and summer months. If you think I have been bitten, keep me quiet and calm and take me to the vet as a matter of urgency. If you see the snake attack make a note of its markings as this will help the vet administer the correct anti-venom. You can tie a constricting band above the bite to slow the spread of the venom. This should be snug but not too tight.

Symptoms to look out for include:

- A small wound with fang marks
- Swelling of the affected area
- Collapse (though we can recover temporarily)
- Sudden weakness
- Vomiting
- Hypersalivation
- Dilated pupils
- Twitching of the muscles

Fireworks phobia

Frenchies, like all other dogs, hate fireworks. Prevention is the best cure; don't ever take me to a firework display and don't let me outside if you hear fireworks being let off nearby.

The best thing is to avoid creating a phobia in the first place. If you know fireworks are going to be let off in the vicinity of your home, keep me indoors. Take me for a good walk before it gets dark, so that I won't need toilet breaks during the evening. Turn up the volume on the television or the radio to drown out the noise and don't leave me home alone. Stay calm and ignore any bangs to give me the message that this is not something I need to worry about.

You can try de-sensitizing therapies to gradually get me accustomed to strange noises. Suitable sounds can be downloaded online and you play them to me, carefully controlling the volume, starting quietly. This is a slow process and I should not be alarmed at any stage, but get gently acclimatized to hearing the sounds, while you play with me and feed me with this quiet noise in the background. Little by little, over weeks, you can raise the volume and I will learn that this is not a threatening sound.

If my phobia is severe the vet can recommend some natural therapies and possibly pheromone treatments to make me feel more secure. Tranquillizers are a very last resort, but even these won't cure the terror, just make us very sleepy.

Genetic issues

Brachycephalic upper airway obstruction syndrome

This umbrella term covers a number of anatomical abnormalities seen in dogs such as French Bulldogs with a characteristic shortened skull and nose. The bones found in the head of brachycephalic breeds are shorter than those in other dog breeds. However, the tissues inside the skull are not shorter. As a result, these tissues are compressed into a smaller space, which can lead to poor air flow through the nose, back of the throat and the windpipe.

Primary problems are indicated by a narrowing of the nostrils, an overly long and thick soft palette, as well as too much tissue in the back of the throat or in the nasal cavity. Your puppy should be assessed by a vet to see how severely it is affected.

Primary problems can lead to secondary problems as the dog ages and cartilage in the larynx loses its rigidity. Indicators are very noisy breathing either with excitement or exercise, noisy snoring, vomiting or regurgitating our food and collapse.

Vets advise that primary problems are addressed when we are young because secondary problems are harder to treat.

Intervertebral disc disease

The vertebrae in our back and neck are cushioned one from the other by intervertebral discs. If these discs degenerate, they can shift position, resulting in a slipped or ruptured disc. This can happen gradually or can be the result of a jump from a piece of furniture. It is very painful and the dog's movement will be impaired, they can be paralyzed and their bowel and bladder affected. Please see a vet immediately. Treatment may require confining the dog in a small space for up to six weeks with very short lead walks permitted and treating them with anti-inflammatories to reduce swelling. Surgery can be successful if undertaken promptly.

Hemivertebrae

French Bulldogs can be born with deformities of the bones of the spine, which can lead to twisting and compression of the spine, causing pain, incontinence and loss of limb function in our back legs. The symptoms can be seen in puppies and diagnosed by X-ray. Intervention requires major surgery and often there is very little that can be done.

Hip dysplasia

Caused when the hip ball and socket is poorly developed and the joint becomes unstable, signs of dysplasia usually show between 5–18 months old.

   Instances of hip dysplasia are falling. However, even with parental checks, genetics can play a part and dysplasia can still be a problem for Frenchies. Treatment is mostly directed towards preventing further deterioration, reducing inflammation and easing pain. Weight loss can help if obesity is an issue and rest and controlled exercise

Symptoms include:
- Limping and lameness
- Difficulty getting up
- Difficulty walking uphill
- Waddling gait
- Reluctance to exercise or climb stairs

are beneficial. Physiotherapy may be recommended. Surgery can be an option in some cases.

Luxating patella

This occurs when the kneecap – the patella – slips out of place from its femoral groove and moves to one side or the other. It causes considerable pain and should be dealt with promptly so that the condition cannot further deteriorate and lead to arthritis. Unfortunately, Frenchies are susceptible to this congenital condition, and weight gain can aggravate it. Signs to look out for are lameness, obvious pain, an occasional skipping gait and stiffness in the affected limb; it can be seen in puppies. If you see this take me to the vet straight away and inform your breeder.

The eyes

Flat-faced dogs like us Frenchies are prone to a range of eye problems. We have shallow eye sockets, which makes our eyes prominent, but this feature can lead to abnormalities in the structure of the eyelids and our prominent nasal folds can compromise eye health. The good news is that breeders are now being offered screening of breeding pairs for inherited eye disease in the hope of gradually eliminating these defects.

Cherry eye

All dogs have a third eyelid, called a nictitating membrane, which acts a bit like a windscreen wiper helping to keep the eye clean and moist. In Frenchies the gland in the corner of this third eyelid can collapse, leaving a red and swollen lump in the corner of the eye. This is a congenital or hereditary problem that usually shows up in puppies or young dogs. Please take me to the vet as soon as possible. Ointment can help to make me more comfortable but surgery may be required. If it affects one eye there is a good chance that the other will be similarly affected.

Distichiasis

If small eyelashes grow abnormally on the inner surface, or the edge of the eyelid, they irritate the surface of the eye and it becomes sore and inflamed. If this condition is left untreated it can lead to ulceration and blindness. If my eye is inflamed and I am rubbing at my eyes with my paw, please take me to the vet.

Entropion

In this condition the edge of the eyelid can turn in so that the eyelashes rub against the surface of the eye causing discomfort and inflammation. French Bulldogs with their droopy eyelids are susceptible to this condition and it usually starts to cause problems around the age of one. If left untreated, it can cause scarring and blindness, so if you detect a problem please take me to the vet to be checked out.

Corneal ulcers

A number of the eye problems described above can, if ignored, lead to corneal ulcers, but I can also have an accident, get scratched in the eye by a cat or a bramble. Ulcers are painful and if left untreated can cause long term damage to vision. Your vet will prescribe eye drops and ointments, medication and pain relief. You may want to keep me out of direct sunlight for a few weeks as strong light can be uncomfortable.

Hereditary cataracts

This condition is common among French Bulldogs, though again breeders are trying to gradually eliminate the disease. A dog must inherit a copy of the HSF4 gene mutation from each parent if they are to go on to develop the disease

– which first shows when the dogs are quite young and causes gradual loss of sight over a couple of years. If the dog inherits the HSF4 gene mutation from just one parent, they will not go on to develop the disease themselves but will be a carrier, and can pass the faulty gene on to their puppies. Screening and reputable breeding could gradually eliminate this genetic fault over time.

Progressive Retinal Atrophy (PRA)

Tests can determine whether or not dogs carry this mutated gene; Frenchies are not the only breed that is affected by this condition. It can lead to degeneration in vision and, at worst, to blindness. There is no cure for this disease, DNA testing is the best hope for gradual eradication. If I seem to be unsure in the dark or start bumping into things, take me to the vet to be checked.

Index

Further reading

Brown, Lolly, *French Bulldog*, NRB Publishing, 2016

Coile, Caroline, *French Bulldogs*, Sourcebooks, 2015

Moore, Asia, *The Happy French Bulldog*, Worldwide Information Publishing, 2019

Pearce, Paul Allen, *French Bulldog Training*, CreateSpace Independent Publishing Platform, 2015

Saben, Susanne, *French Bulldog: The French Bulldog Bible*, DYM Worldwide Publishers, 2017

Whitwam, Linda, *The French Bulldog Handbook*, CreateSpace Independent Publishing Platform, 2015

Acknowledgements

My thanks must go to Jimmy the Lurcher, our first family dog, who turned this cat-loving, dog-hating mother of two into an ardent dog-worshipper. Jimmy was a living, breathing incarnation of a badly-behaved dog and together we discovered how dog training can transform your life.

Every dog owner will get to know numerous French Bulldogs as they walk their dogs, for they are great socialites. I must thank my Kent chum Tracey Wilson for giving me the chance to get to know her Frenchie, Ted. He and my whippet puppy Betsey conducted a passionate love affair, though two less obviously compatible companions it would be hard to find. Tracey trusted me with dog-sitting duties and Ted inducted me in the charms of Frenchie ownership. Tracey has spent long hours discussing the pros and cons of Frenchie ownership with me and patiently answered my many queries.

I had the pleasure of meeting the Frenchie, Sidney, at a party where she worked the room very efficiently, meeting and greeting all the humans, in the company of her owner Nancy-May Hingston. Nancy-May also kindly discussed the pleasures and perils of Frenchie ownership with me. I must also thank the many nameless French Bulldog owners who tolerated a bombardment of queries from a complete stranger and who allowed me to pet their pooches.

I must thank my husband Eric, without whose patient nagging I would never have discovered that dog-owning was a good thing. Our children, Florence and Teddy, have patiently endured their parents' dog-worshipping tendencies and embraced the delights of dog walking in the rain. They are the first to point out if the house ever smells of dog, so keep me on my domestic toes, and are quick to highlight any pungent emissions of canine wind.

At Batsford I must, as always, thank Polly Powell for her faith in me. Lilly Phelan has been the kindest and gentlest of editors and a delight to work with and Gemma Doyle must be thanked for her superb design.